One Heart, One Mind

Walking with God Day by Day

A Catholic Bible Study

By Rich Cleveland

One Heart, One Mind is the first of a series of Scripture-based small-group discussion books developed to be used within Catholic communities. These materials were developed, field-tested, and successfully used through the Small Catholic Communities at Holy Apostles Catholic Church in Colorado Springs, Colorado.

These materials are designed to provide foundational training in both personal spirituality and the ability to participate successfully in a small group. Participants learn to enjoy daily Bible reading and prayer and to make these disciplines a significant resource in their relationship with Christ. Regular meditation on Scripture and meaningful participation in discussion of the Scriptures are developed as other valuable disciplines. These disciplines are nourished in a loving, caring environment that can lead to a motivating, caring Christian community.

These booklets incorporate reflection on Scripture passages around various important topics of personal spirituality and discipleship. Each discussion topic is presented and reinforced by references to valuable Catholic resources.

A leader's guide is available to provide facilitators with resource suggestions for handling the various sessions and creating helpful small-group dynamics. This guide is available as a free download at www.emmausjourney.org.

Emmaus Journey is an evangelization and discipleship ministry of The Navigators, an interdenominational religious organization, conducted in and through Catholic parishes.

Table of Contents

I would like to recommend for your consideration and use these Emmaus Journey Scripture discussion materials. These studies were developed within the Holy Apostles Parish Small Catholic Communities ministry and honor both the value of Scripture reflection and respect for Catholic faith, culture, and tradition.

Go and Make Disciples, published by the National Council of Catholic Bishops, suggests as Goal 1: "To bring about in all Catholics such an enthusiasm for their faith that, in living their faith in Jesus, they freely share it with others." These Emmaus Journey materials were designed for, and help accomplish, this goal. The following objectives, which *Go and Make Disciples* recommends, are furthered through these studies:

- "To foster an experience of conversion and renewal in the heart of every believer, leading to a more active living of Catholic life."
- "To foster an appreciation of God's word in the lives of all Catholics."
- "To foster a renewed understanding of the faith among Catholics."
- "To foster a sense of discipleship among Catholic adults . . ."
- "To foster active and personal religious experience through participation in small-group and communal experiences in which the Good News is shared, experienced and applied to daily life."

The author, Rich Cleveland, has developed the Small Catholic Communities ministry at Holy Apostles Parish for four years. I have experienced our parishioners coming alive in their Catholic faith through these Emmaus Journey materials. I pray that God will use these materials to further his life and work among you and your group.

Sincerely,

Fr. Paul Wicker
Pastor
Holy Apostles Catholic Church

Session 1

Introduction

Before You Begin

Get acquainted with the others in your group by sharing your answers to these questions:

- **What is your name?**
- **What is your occupation?**
- **What is your favorite vacation activity?**

Personal spirituality and Christian community do not usually happen by accident. In fact, these ideas are contrary to our natural tendencies and the way the world normally thinks. Both require significant commitment, planned development, and consistent practice. Both are encouraged by Christ and the Scriptures. And, not surprisingly, both are opposed by the "spiritual forces of evil." Consequently, believers must depend on God's grace to develop their personal spirituality and real Christian community.

The materials you will use in the months ahead are designed to introduce you to several practical skills. They will enhance your personal spiritual growth and your ability to participate in community with other Christians. Some tools and habits may be new to you, but they all have been developed and used by Catholics with very positive results.

Change can be either fearsome or wonderful, resisted or embraced. In Christ, change can be readily embraced as a wonderful, necessary process. Paul says in 2 Corinthians 3:16-18: "When one turns to the Lord, the veil is removed. Now the Lord is the Spirit, and where the Spirit of the Lord is, there is freedom. And all of us, with unveiled faces, seeing the glory of the Lord as though reflected in a mirror, are being transformed into the same image from one degree of glory to another; for this comes from the Lord, the Spirit."

This transformation Paul talks about means change. So as you discover new concepts, tools, and experiences, ask God to help you embrace them as part of the wonderful transformation he has for you.

What to Expect

Early on, you will be introduced to skills and experiences that may be new to you. These skills—daily Scripture reading, Bible study preparation, weekly sharing, conversational prayer—are the building blocks of personal spirituality and Christian community.

The group facilitator will provide direction and discussion-group stimulation, and will introduce new material with some instruction. But basically, the success of the group is dependent upon your preparation, wholehearted participation, and open sharing with others in the group.

During the first two weeks, the group will read through new material together. This will keep you from having to take copious notes or from missing important points. It also encourages everyone to participate and overcome their natural shyness in a new group.

In later sessions, your group will be encouraged to talk about how Christ has been involved in your lives, to share from your daily reading, to discuss the Bible study material, to pray, and to socialize together. Within the first few weeks, this small Catholic community will likely become a vital part of your life.

Daily Bible Reading and Prayer

> We have, however, the words of Scripture to which to pay attention. A psalm, a parable, a biblical story, a saying of Jesus, or a word of Paul, Peter, James, Jude, or John can help us focus our attention on God's presence. When we place words from the Scriptures in the center of our solitude, such words—whether a short expression, a few sentences, or a longer text—can function as the point to which we return when we have wandered off in different directions. They form a safe anchoring place in a stormy sea.
> —Henri J. M. Nouwen, *Making All Things New: An Invitation to Spiritual Life,* p. 77

One of the best investments you can make is to spend time each day with Jesus through reading the Scriptures and praying. People who have developed this habit have seen the difference daily Scripture reading and praying make in their relationship with God. Here are just a few of the ways daily Scripture reading can affect your life.

Communion with Jesus. Communication with Jesus becomes more vital and concrete when you intentionally take time to meet with him through reading the Scriptures and praying. God intentionally planned fellowship with us, as Paul explains in 1 Corinthians 1:9: "God is faithful; by him you were called into the fellowship of his Son, Jesus Christ our Lord."

As you read and meditate on Scripture, God will communicate to you things that are important to him. Jesus promised, "The Advocate, the Holy Spirit, whom the Father will send in my name, will teach you everything, and remind you of all that I have said to you" (John 14:26). Also,

"When we place words from the Scriptures in the center of our solitude, such words—whether a short expression, a few sentences, or a longer text—can function as the point to which we return when we have wandered off in different directions." —Henri Nouwen

daily prayer enables you to talk to God about what's important to you—as well as what is important to him.

Life Transformation. Over time, reading Scripture will transform your mental, emotional, and spiritual life, and will positively affect the choices you make. The psalmist, in Psalm 19:7-11 (NAB 8-12), expressed this benefit of reading and obeying the Scriptures:

> The law of the LORD is perfect, reviving the soul;
> the decrees of the LORD are sure, making wise the simple;
> the precepts of the LORD are right, rejoicing the heart;
> the commandment of the LORD is clear, enlightening the eyes;
> the fear of the LORD is pure, enduring forever;
> the ordinances of the LORD are true and righteous altogether.
> More to be desired are they than gold, even much fine gold;
> sweeter also than honey, and drippings of the honeycomb.
> Moreover by them is your servant warned;
> in keeping them there is great reward.

Scripture reading helps clarify your thinking and perspective on life. The Scriptures give direction and guidance for daily living. And as your relationship with the Lord grows through your study of the Bible, you will experience new levels of joy and confidence in your life. Also, giving a small amount of your undivided attention to Christ each day provides tremendous long-range benefits as your life is graciously and gradually transformed.

Practical Methods for Daily Scripture Reading

Many of us have heard or voiced frustration over Scripture reading: "I've tried reading the Bible, but I can't get anything out of it." By following a few simple and practical suggestions, you will discover that reading the Bible can be fun, spiritually invigorating, and extremely meaningful. The following Scripture reading methods have proven to be very helpful in making your Scripture reading experience come alive:

• Reading and marking	Session 1
• Reading plan	Session 1
• Relating your spiritual journey to others	Session 1
• Relying on the Holy Spirit	Session 1
• Responding in prayer	Session 2
• Recording one key thought	Session 3

Reading and Marking

1. Use an inexpensive Bible with language and style that are new and refreshing to you. Most Catholic or religious bookstores carry a variety of paperback Catholic translations or paraphrases. Be sure that you're comfortable with the translation's accuracy as well as its language.

2. Follow an annual Bible-reading plan so you know what to read each day. With a reading plan, you will easily be able to see your progress. In this book, you will find two kinds of reading plans—one based on the daily Lectionary readings, and one that will lead you through consecutive chapters of the Bible.

Reading through individual books of the Bible enables you to grasp the context of Scripture more broadly. To begin, simply choose a book of the Bible you'd like to read. Determine how much of the book you want to read each day or how long you want to read each day. Draw a line through the appropriate box on the Daily Scripture Reading Record (found on page 109) as you finish each chapter. You may want to consider a goal of reading through the entire Bible during a two- or three-year period.

With the daily Lectionary reading plan, you will be able to follow the Scripture passages used in the daily Mass. There are several lectionary-based reading plans available. With this course we offer two suggestions. At the Emmaus Journey website (emmausjourney.org) you can download a free three-month Lectionary Reading Record in a format similar to the one found on page 109. This record is used in a similar way. You begin reading at the appropriate week of the Liturgical Year. As you finish the day's readings, check off the corresponding boxes on the reading record.

A Lectionary-based reading plan is also available by ordering *The Word Among Us*. This magazine provides all of the Scripture references for each day, plus a stimulating meditation on one of the passages for each day.

3. As you read your Bible, mark the passages that are especially meaningful to you. The more you mark, the more you'll think and interact with the Scriptures. Conversely, as you mark less, you may find yourself becoming drowsy or having to reread passages to grasp their meaning. Don't be afraid that you're marking too much in your Bible. This technique is crucial for you to understand what you're reading.

Relating Your Spiritual Journey to Others

It is important to share with others, preferably on a weekly basis, what you are discovering. This, too, will help you clarify your thoughts. As you share a thought with someone else, you will see that it makes an even more significant and lasting impression on you. This poem is a helpful reminder:

Thoughts disentangle themselves
when they pass over the lips
and through the fingertips.

As you share your discoveries with others, your thoughts will be reinforced, and they will provide additional spiritual stimulation. Furthermore, God is able to use what you share to encourage and help those listening. Paul wrote in Romans 10:17: "Faith comes from what is heard, and what is heard comes through the word of Christ." Often what you share will be instrumental in strengthening not only your own faith, but also the faith of others. (But remember to share what the Holy Spirit impressed on your own life, not something you hope God will impress on someone else in the group.)

Since, as 2 Peter 1:20 warns, "No prophecy of scripture is a matter of one's own interpretation," sharing your thoughts with other believers provides an opportunity for them to respond with their own insights. This interaction over God's word helps you to grow and learn from others and to remain on track doctrinally.

Relying on the Holy Spirit

One of the most important principles of daily Scripture reading and prayer is reliance on the Holy Spirit for help. Reading the Bible can become sterile and meaningless when you do it on your own. And when the Holy Spirit is not invited into your devotional life, you run the risk of developing pride in your own Bible knowledge or in your self-discipline.

Understanding Scripture is a spiritual gift, a grace dependent on the Holy Spirit. Paul says in 1 Corinthians 2:10-12: "These things God has revealed to us through the Spirit; for the Spirit searches everything, even the depths of God. For what human being knows what is truly human except the human spirit that is within? So also no one comprehends what is truly God's except the Spirit of God. Now we have received not the spirit of the world, but the Spirit that is from God, so that we may understand the gifts bestowed on us by God."

Before you begin reading each day, humbly ask the Holy Spirit to illuminate your mind and condition your heart to receive what God has for you in his word.

Reading and Marking Your Bible Exercise

Read the following passage and mark those things you find helpful or interesting. Move through the passage at a comfortable and thoughtful pace. Don't worry about completing the entire passage during this exercise.

2 Peter 1:3-15

[3] His divine power has given us everything needed for life and godliness, through the knowledge of him who called us by his own glory and goodness. [4] Thus he has given us, through these things, his precious and very great promises, so that through them you may escape from the corruption that is in the world because of lust, and may become participants of the divine nature. [5] For this very reason, you must make every effort to support your faith with goodness, and goodness with knowledge, [6] and knowledge with self-control, and self-control with endurance, and endurance with godliness, [7] and godliness with mutual affection, and mutual affection with love. [8] For if these things are yours and are increasing among you, they keep you from being ineffective and unfruitful in the knowledge of our Lord Jesus Christ.
[9] For anyone who lacks these things is nearsighted and blind, and is forgetful of the cleansing of past sins. [10] Therefore, brothers and sisters, be all the more eager to confirm your call and election, for if you do this, you will never stumble. [11] For in this way, entry into the eternal kingdom of our Lord and Savior Jesus Christ will be richly provided for you.

[12] Therefore I intend to keep on reminding you of these things, though you know them already and are established in the truth that has come to you. [13] I think it right, as long as I am in this body, to refresh your memory, [14] since I know that my death will come soon, as indeed our Lord Jesus Christ has made clear to me. [15] And I will make every effort so that after my departure you may be able at any time to recall these things.

Preparation for Session 2

1. Purchase an inexpensive Bible to use for your daily reading.
2. Choose which reading plan you would prefer to use and record your progress daily.
3. Begin daily reading and marking a designated portion of Scripture.
4. Read "Responding in Prayer" on pages 22-27, and mark those parts which you feel are important.

Notes for Session 1

Notes for Session 1

Session 2

Responding in Prayer

Before You Begin

Get acquainted with the others in your group by sharing your answers to these questions:
- **What is your name?**
- **What size was your family?**
- **What is your favorite hobby?**

Share insights from your daily Bible reading.

There are several ways to find nourishment and help through Scripture. Last week we looked at daily reading and meditating on a Scripture passage while marking what we read. This casual daily reading provides a refreshing stroll through the Bible. This approach gives an overview while allowing God to impress various truths on your heart, providing daily encouragement, guidance, and challenge.

Hearing God's word read and taught is another important and fruitful approach. St. Paul says in Romans: "Faith comes from what is heard, and what is heard comes through the word of Christ" (10:17).

As Scripture is read, we often are able to hear truth in a new way. The Holy Spirit uses the spoken word to minister to us. As Scripture is taught, we open ourselves to truth and allow God to speak to us through another person's preparation. This is one reason why attendance at Mass is so crucial to our spiritual health. As we listen with attentive hearts to the reading of God's word and its amplification during the homily, the Holy Spirit is able to minister to us in unexpected and meaningful ways.

Bible study and discussion is yet another way to be nourished by Scripture. By studying portions of Scripture topically or chapter-by-chapter, we are able to give more thoughtful consideration to Bible passages. This allows us to:

- explore important truths more deeply and in context.
- form and strengthen godly convictions and values.
- carefully consider the practical implications of these truths.

In addition, Bible study discussion provides:

- weekly motivation to prepare and study.
- a pleasant and constructive environment in which we can learn from one another.
- "checks and balances" against wrong and harmful interpretation.
- encouragement to align our lives with the truth of God's word.

So far, you've learned that daily Scripture reading is used by God to communicate to us what is important to him. One of the Holy Spirit's responsibilities is to "teach you everything, and remind you of all that I have said to you" (John 14:26). However, as you meet with Christ through the reading of the Scriptures, you also bring to your communion your hopes and dreams, hurts and sorrows, questions and gratitude—all of which are important to you.

Sometimes you may not make the connection between God's concerns and your own. It's easy to ignore talking to God about the things that are important to him and instead concentrate only on your own concerns.

To achieve more balance in your communication with God, try these suggestions:

1. Consciously review what you have read and marked to crystallize in your mind what the Holy Spirit has impressed on your heart. Frequently, when reviewing like this, you will find a trend in your reading and in God's communication with you.

2. In a simple and direct way, without fear or hesitancy, talk to God about what his Spirit has revealed to you through the Scriptures. It is important to talk to God about what is important to him. You also need to talk to him about the people and situations that are on your heart.

3. There are many ways to pray about the same passage, depending on where you are in life's journey. When you pray, it may be helpful to remember the acrostic "ACTS," which stands for Adoration, Confession, Thanksgiving, and Supplication.

Adoration. Express to God your love, honor, and admiration in reverence and worship. In your daily Scripture reading, you often will discover a fresh aspect of God, Jesus, or the Holy Spirit that elicits your adoration. Your love, honor, admiration, and affection can be expressed verbally through words or song, or by reciting a scriptural passage of praise and adoration, such as 1 Chronicles 29:11-12: "Yours, O LORD, are the greatness, the power, the glory, the victory, and the majesty; for all that is in the heavens and on the earth is yours; yours is the kingdom, O LORD, and you are exalted as head above all. Riches and honor come from you, and you rule over all. In your hand are power and might; and it is in your hand to make great and to give strength to all."

You also can express your feelings to God through a learned prayer of praise, such as the Gloria:

Glory to God in the highest, and peace to his people on earth.
Lord God, Heavenly King, Almighty God, and Father,
we worship you, we give you thanks, we praise you for your glory.
Lord Jesus Christ, only Son of the Father, Lord God, Lamb of God,
you take away the sin of the world: have mercy on us;
you are seated at the right hand of the Father: receive our prayer.
For you alone are the Holy One, you alone are the Lord,
you alone are the Most High, Jesus Christ,
with the Holy Spirit, in the glory of God the Father. Amen.

Confession. As you reflect on your attitudes and actions in light of God's word, you may become aware of failings, shortcomings, and sin. God does not want you to carry around these feelings of guilt throughout the day or until you are able to participate in the Rite of Reconciliation. He established repentance, confession, and assurance of forgiveness as the means of dealing with the guilt and sorrow you feel. Include in your confession the "three R's":

Recognize and acknowledge to God that some specific behavior or attitude has been unacceptable to him.

Receive by faith the forgiveness available in Christ. He has promised, "If we confess our sins, he who is faithful and just will forgive us our sins and cleanse us from all unrighteousness" (1 John 1:9).

Repent, which means to willfully abandon the unacceptable behavior or attitudes the Holy Spirit has identified to us.

Thanksgiving. To maintain your perspective and joy, express your gratitude to God for his involvement in your life. Giving thanks helps you focus on the many benefits and blessings you have in Christ. It takes your mind off your concerns and problems. The Scriptures often will reveal to you a reason to give thanks. Then, when you are praying for your concerns, you are able to view your situation not simply as your own inadequacy, but with hope based on God's adequacy to meet your every need.

Supplication. God encourages you to humbly and earnestly ask him to meet your needs and other people's needs. At times, as you read the Scriptures, you will discover a truth you would like to claim for yourself or someone else. God wants you to ask him for great, important things as well as simple, everyday things. Jesus challenged his disciples: "If you ask anything of the Father in my name, he will give it to you . . . Ask and you will receive, so that your joy may be complete" (John 16:23-24).

> At the end of such a period of quiet dwelling with God we may, through intercessory prayer, lead all the people who are part of our lives, friends as well as enemies, into his healing presence.
> —Henri J.M. Nouwen, *Making All Things New,* p.78

As you use ACTS to shape your prayer, you will find your prayer life becoming broader. You will be able to pray for people and situations in new ways.

Consider these suggestions as you pray for the people and concerns in your life:

- Jot down the names of people and situations for whom you feel responsible to pray.

- Pray specifically rather than simply asking God to "bless" someone or something.

- Recruit other believers to pray about a specific request with you. Because people have so many of their own concerns to pray about, ask them to join with you in prayer now rather than asking them to add you to their "prayer list."

When you see God answer your specific request, remember to thank him. Share God's gracious answer with friends so that their faith will be strengthened as well.

Preparation for Session 3

1. Continue reading and marking your Bible daily, recording your progress on your reading record.

2. Read "Using a Spiritual Journal" on pages 30-32, and mark the points that you feel are important or interesting for you.

Notes for Session 2

Notes for Session 2

Notes for Session 2

Session 3

Using a Spiritual Journal

Before You Begin

Share insights from your daily Bible reading.

One way to make your daily Scripture reading refreshing and practical is to record each day how one key thought captured your attention. Elaborating on one thought that stood out to you will help you grasp its meaning more concretely. Remember the poem:

Thoughts disentangle themselves
when they pass over the lips
and through the fingertips.

Recording your thoughts will:

- Motivate you and help you see progress in your spiritual journey.
- Discipline you to think concretely about what the Holy Spirit is showing you.
- Enable you to remember and think throughout the day about God's word and its meaning for your life.
- Frequently provide just the right thought to share with someone who needs spiritual encouragement.
- Provide, over time, a record of how the Holy Spirit has spoken to you. During a personal retreat or a day of reflection, you can review

these thoughts to discover trends that provide new motivation, direction, and challenge.

At the end of this study you will find "Spiritual Journal" forms for daily recording one or more reflections from your daily reading and prayer. Each day, record the passage from which your reflection comes. Then write your thoughts about the passage.

Remember that you are writing for your own benefit and not to impress others. Your recorded thoughts don't have to be profound. Actually, most "profound" things are profound in their simplicity. Try consistently to record at least one thought, even on days when your reading is less exciting to you.

Finally, remember that these methods (reading and marking your Bible, using a daily reading plan, responding in prayer to the passage, and recording a key thought in a spiritual journal) are designed to enhance your daily reading and prayer. Don't be legalistic, arrogant, or defeated by your consistency or lack of it. Consistency comes by starting fresh each time you feel you have failed. Don't forget that fellowship with Christ should be enjoyable!

Journaling Exercise

Choose a passage from this week's daily Bible reading and write about how this thought impressed you. During discussion time, you will have an opportunity to share your thoughts with others.

This week, share first from the "Spiritual Journal" form you completed.

During the next four weeks you, along with the other members of the group, will be sharing primarily from your daily Scripture reading. Sociologists tell us that it takes a minimum of fourteen days to break a habit, such as failing to read God's word, and a minimum of another fourteen days to establish a new habit, such as reading God's word and praying to him. So one objective of the remaining four weeks is to get well established in this new habit.

Consequently, it will be important for you to be as consistent as possible. Your minimum goal should be to read the Scriptures and pray at least five times a week. Some people, in their enthusiasm and in light of the above information, have determined to read the Scriptures and pray daily for fourteen consecutive days, without missing. They started the fourteen consecutive days beginning with this lesson. Those who missed a day started over until they reached their goal. Needless to say, though these people did not maintain this more legalistic objective indefinitely, they did establish a lifetime habit that proved to be both enjoyable and spiritually profitable.

Additionally, we will introduce some complementary material that will provide some variety and insight for your devotional life.

Preparation for Session 4

1. Continue to read and mark your Bible daily, and record your progress on your reading record.

2. After completing your daily Scripture reading, record at least one reflection in your Spiritual Journal on pages 33-39.

3. Read and mark the information on *Lectio Divina* and be prepared to share your impressions.

Spiritual Journal

Passage:____**Date:**______

Day 1

Spiritual Journal

Passage:____Date:______

Day 2

Spiritual Journal

Passage:____Date:______

Day 3

Spiritual Journal

Passage:______________________________ **Date:**______

Day 4

Spiritual Journal

Passage:____ **Date:**_______

Day 5

Spiritual Journal

Passage:____**Date:**______

Day 6

Spiritual Journal

Passage:____**Date:**______

Day 7

Notes for Session 3

Notes for Session 3

Session 4

Lectio Divina

Before You Begin

Share insights from your daily Bible reading.

Lectio Divina is a centuries-old approach to meditating on the Scriptures that still offers us pertinent insights for our lives today. Saint Benedict is usually credited with articulating and encouraging the value of *Lectio Divina* through his Rule for monastic life. Benedict believed that meditating on Scripture and prayer were at the heart of a life dedicated to Christ. Consequently, he not only included this emphasis within his monastic rule but also recommended a process of Scripture meditation that many thousands of lay people have found very helpful.

Not totally unlike the methods you have already learned in this material, *Lectio Divina* normally involves four levels of interaction with God through the Scriptures: reading, meditation, prayer, and contemplation. Though these four levels of interaction are listed in order, as you become more comfortable with this process you will undoubtedly find your reading simultaneously interspersed with deeper meditation and responsive prayer, in a way similar to that which we have discussed previously.

In the next two sessions we want to explore more deeply some practical ways of reading, meditating, and prayer. We won't provide any practical suggestions for contemplation inasmuch as contemplation is not so much something you *do*, as it is something you *experience* as you grow in meditation and prayer. So let's begin by discussing reading God's word.

Scripture Reading

In the book *Sacred Reading*, Michael Casey attributes the following quote to Abba Poeman, a desert father: "The nature of water is soft, that of stone is hard; but if a bottle is hung above the stone, allowing the water to fall drop by drop, it wears away the stone. So it is with the word of God; it is soft and our heart is hard, but the [one] who hears the word of God often, opens his heart to the fear of God. (p.10)

It is our hope that by now you have already developed a deep appreciation for reading God's word. However, there are several things you can do to enhance Scripture reading and meditation.

1. **Prepare Your Heart.** Being busy, it is easy through discipline to jump into our daily reading and prayer without much preparation. We all have done it and can attest to its lesser degree of effectiveness, for reading God's word is not the same as reading any other book. Consequently, it is very helpful to sit or kneel for a couple of minutes in silence and quietness before God, acknowledging his presence.

   Many have found it helpful to invite the Holy Spirit's enlightenment by reciting a prayer similar to the following: "Search me, O God, and know my heart; test me and know my thoughts. See if there is any wicked way in me, and lead me in the way everlasting" (Psalm 139:23-24).

2. **Read Aloud.** Sometimes because of tiredness or mental distraction we find that we have read a portion of Scripture and yet remain oblivious to what we have just read. Perhaps we even find ourselves

dozing off. Marking your Bible as you read is a method you have already learned and may have found helpful for remaining attentive. However, another effective way to combat these problems is to read the Scriptures aloud.

When you read Scripture aloud it involves more of your senses. Not only do your eyes see the words and your mind comprehend them, but also your mouth must be engaged to form and speak the words, and your ears must be attentive to hear them spoken. Using more senses makes a deeper impression on your mind and requires you to be more alert. If you try to read the words as you think they might actually have been spoken, you will also find your emotions more actively involved as you capture the intent and inflection of the speaker.

3. **Use a different translation than one to which you are accustomed.** This can help you meditate more deeply. Different translations provide various ways of stating passages with which you are familiar and can cause you to see a new facet of truth that you have previously overlooked. It is always helpful to have your usual, "reliable" translation available also so that you can compare passages. Many people also find it beneficial to actually write out the passage in their own words so that they can fully capture their understanding of what it is saying.

4. **Memorize Scripture.** This can enable you to extend the impact of your daily Scripture reading throughout the day. Joshua 1:8 says: "This book of the law shall not depart out of your mouth; you shall meditate on it day and night, so that you may be careful to act in accordance with all that is written in it. For then you shall make your

way prosperous, and then you shall be successful." Most of us cannot meditate on Scripture day and night, but we can commit key passages to memory and meditate on them. As we review and reflect on them at different points during the day when our mind would normally be idle (or occupied with less honorable thoughts), we can turn our attention to God and his word. As we meditate on God's word more frequently, our lives become anchored in him and in turn we will experience spiritual prosperity and success.

Here is a simple method you can use.

- Choose one passage of Scripture from your previous week's reading that is particularly meaningful to you.
- Write out the verse on a small card, perhaps on a business card blank that you can purchase at an office supply store, or on half a 3x5 card.
- On the first day, learn the passage well enough to be able to say it from memory, and that evening go to sleep reviewing the verse in your mind. You'll be amazed how often you will wake in the morning thinking about God's word.
- Recall, review, and meditate on the verse several times during each day of the week when you have time on your hands, such as waiting for an appointment, sitting in traffic, eating your lunch, etc.

Try to incorporate several of these simple methods during the coming week to see how they will enhance your reading and meditation on God's word.

Preparation for Session 5

1. Continue to read and mark your Bible daily, and record your progress on your reading record.

2. After completing your daily Scripture reading each day, record at least one reflection in your Spiritual Journal on pages 47-54.

3. Read and mark the information on *Lectio Divina* and be prepared to share what you found helpful.

Spiritual Journal

Passage:____**Date:**______

Day 1

Spiritual Journal

Passage:____**Date:**______

Day 2

Spiritual Journal

Passage:____ **Date:**_______

Day 3

Spiritual Journal

Passage:____**Date:**______

Day 4

Spiritual Journal

Passage:____ **Date:**______

Day 5

Spiritual Journal

Passage:____ Date:______

Day 6

Spiritual Journal

Passage:____ **Date:**______

Day 7

Notes for Session 4

Notes for Session 4

Session 5

Lectio Divina (Cont.)

Before You Begin

Share insights from your daily Bible reading.

Prayer is very much at the heart of *Lectio Divina* and is perhaps one of the most often neglected aspects of our lives as Christians. St. Francis de Sales, in *Introduction to the Devout Life,* effectively explains the critical importance of prayer:

> Since prayer places our intellect in the brilliance of God's light and exposes our will to the warmth of his heavenly love, nothing else so effectively purifies our intellect of ignorance and our will of depraved affections. It is a stream of holy water that flows forth and makes the plants of our good desires grow green and flourish and quenches the passions within our hearts.—*The Neccesity of Prayer,* p.81

Reading and meditating on Scripture without including an element of prayer can cause our faith to become purely academic. We can know a lot of information about Jesus and the Christian life and yet incorporate very little into our life without prayer. Prayer enables us to personalize the meaning of Scripture and allow it to influence our relationship with God as well as affect our behavior. The great mystic, Brother

Lawrence, described prayer this way: "I picture myself as a piece of stone before a sculptor who intends to make a statue out if it. Presenting myself like this before the Lord, I beg him to form in my soul his perfect image and make me wholly like Christ" (from *Walking with the Father,* p.117).

Fortunately, because of the presence of the Holy Spirit, and the freedom we have to come into his presence at any time as God's children, our prayer life doesn't have to be stymied because of limited time. We can take a few minutes each morning to read and meditate on God's word, and commune with the Father in prayer. Then throughout the day we can continue our communication with the Father, praying from the heart, and sharing our day and our life with him in prayer. It is not the *quantity* of time in prayer that affects our spiritual life, but rather the *quality*. Consequently, during these days when you are developing these spiritual habits, don't worry about the time. Focus instead on having quality communication with God.

Here are some practical suggestions for enhancing your prayer time:

- Often when we have a limited amount of time and need to leave for work or have some other time frame we are concerned about, our prayer is interrupted by having to monitor our watches. You will find it helpful to set an egg timer or watch alarm to ring at the end of the time you have available for prayer. Then forget about the clock and immerse yourself in prayer.

- Arranging a prayer space can help create an environment conducive to prayer. A crucifix, a meaningful picture, a safely lit candle, and a comfortable place to kneel or sit—all of these can help you enter into an atmosphere of prayer. This place will become a sacred space that enhances your communion with God.

- Music can also help establish an environment of prayer. Listening to one or two well selected, worshipful songs before our prayer time can lift our hearts in praise and adoration. It is even better yet, to sing to God of our love. Though our voice may not be great, God will rejoice to see and hear us singing words of love and devotion to him, and it will encourage us to express our affection for him.

- Separate your intercessory prayer from the prayer that evolves out of your reading and meditation. Both are valuable, but praying for people and things in our lives usually overrides and crowds out prayer of adoration and reflection. Consider the prayer that arises from your reading and meditation to be your primary preoccupation and an opportunity for quiet, intimate discussion with your Lord and the lover of your soul.

- Lastly, audible prayer seems to be more beneficial than silent prayer (though God can hear either). By praying aloud we not only use more of our senses, as we spoke about in previous sessions, but it tends to make our prayers more concrete. Even if the prayer is only softly spoken due to others being in close proximity to us, it will usually make our prayer more meaningful. Or you might consider slowing down your prayer time to compose in writing a prayer to God which will cause you to choose words that reflect your heart. Many of the prayers we have memorized and recite have come from saints who have simply composed in writing their prayer to God. To begin with you might try to communicate aloud to God during your prayer and once a week write out a prayer to God.

Try some of these suggestions during this coming week to enhance the quality of your prayer time. Joseph Cardinal Bernardin commented in *The Gift of Peace,* "Lord, I know that I spend a certain amount of that morning hour of prayer daydreaming, problem-solving, and I'm not sure

"Lord, I know that I spend a certain amount of that morning hour of prayer daydreaming, problem-solving, and I'm not sure that I can cut that out. I'll try, but the important thing is, I'm not going to give that time to anybody else." — Joseph Cardinal Bernardin

Photograph by Michael L. Abramson

that I can cut that out. I'll try, but the important thing is, I'm not going to give that time to anybody else. So even though it may not unite me with you as much as it should, nobody else is going to get that time." So don't fret and worry, always assessing the quality of your prayer. Remember that you are on a journey of a lifetime. The important thing is that though the progress may be slow, you are still making steady progress on your spiritual journey.

Preparation for Session 6

1. Continue to read and mark your Bible daily, and record your progress on your reading record.

2. After completing your daily Scripture reading each day, record at least one reflection in your Spiritual Journal on pages 61-67 (Note: Next week's session purposely does not have a lot of supplemental material so that more time can be devoted to sharing from your daily reading. So please come prepared to share several times.)

3. Read and mark the information on "The Cumulative Effect," and be prepared to share what you found helpful.

4. Complete the mid-course evaluation.

Spiritual Journal

Passage:____ **Date:**______

Day 1

Spiritual Journal

Passage:____**Date:**______

Day 2

Spiritual Journal

Passage:____ **Date:**______

Day 3

Spiritual Journal

Passage:____**Date:**______

Day 4

Spiritual Journal

Passage:____**Date:**________

Day 5

Spiritual Journal

Passage:____**Date:**______

Day 6

Spiritual Journal

Passage:____**Date:**______

Day 7

Notes for Session 5

Notes for Session 5

The Cumulative Effect

Before You Begin

Share insights from your daily Bible reading.

Cardinal Jean Marie Lustiger, in the book, *Dare to Believe* is quoted as saying: "What you, Christians, must do is to acquire this Gospel as your mother tongue and to take as your own the history to which you are the heirs; otherwise you become lost children. This cannot happen without work. The word of God must become your mother tongue, must inspire your heart, dwell in your spirit, nourish your life; this familiarity with God which keeps us in his church must become the very heart of your life."

These are profound and compelling words regarding our responsibility to God's word. The challenge to acquire God's word fully implies both *knowing* it thoroughly and *believing* it ardently. Compelling though these words may be, for many they also become frustrating, for we wonder, "How can I, a busy layperson, fully acquire God's word? Wouldn't I have to quit and go off to seminary?" Fortunately, we can reply to this question, "No. The alternative is amazingly simple—the cumulative effect."

Imagine if someone told you that to acquire God's word fully you would need to spend fifty-two hours reading, meditating, and praying over the Scriptures every year. You would probably think they were crazy and protest that you had a job and family and could not afford to take the time to do so. Yet if you will spend just fifteen minutes a day doing this, and if you only do it four days a week, at the end of one year you will have spent fifty-two hours reading and thinking about God's word. That is one of the greatest values of daily Bible reading and prayer. It has a cumulative effect. It is very much like taking a fistful of snow, forming a little snowball, and beginning to roll it on the ground. Though it only acquires a little snow with each roll, before long the cumulative effect results in a giant snowball. So it is with the cumulative effect that comes from investing a little time each day reading and meditating on the Bible and praying about what you have read. The consistent habit of daily reading, meditating, and praying on Scripture, day after day, will make God's word your "mother tongue" and have a major impact on your heart and spirit, giving you such "familiarity with God" that he will "become the very heart of your life."

Preparation for Session 7

1. Continue to read and mark your Bible daily, and record your progress on your reading record.

2. After completing your daily Scripture reading each day, record at least one reflection in your Spiritual Journal on pages 73-79.

3. Read and mark the information on "Setting Spiritual Goals" and complete the exercise on pages 82-85.

Mid-Course Evaluation

In a few short weeks we will have completed *One Heart, One Mind*. Hopefully everyone will be interested in continuing with the small group into the booklet *Embracing the Kingdom*. Nevertheless, this is a good point to evaluate how we are responding to the things we are learning. For whether we continue into the next booklet or not, the truth and techniques we have discovered should become a significant part of our lives.

What, for you, has been the most beneficial aspect of the material?

____

____

____

____

____

What has been the most difficult aspect to put into practice?

____

____

____

____

____

How do you feel about committing to read the Scriptures and pray each day?

____

____

____

____

____

We all experience the tension between the push to be faithful to new values and convictions and the pull back to our old habits and lifestyles. Which do you think will have the biggest influence on you? Why?

____

____

____

____

____

What is the most important thing you could do to insure that the daily reading of Scripture and prayer will become a normal part of your day?

____

____

____

____

____

Spiritual Journal

Passage:____ Date:______

Day 1

Spiritual Journal

Passage:____Date:_____

Day 2

Spiritual Journal

Passage:____**Date:**______

Day 3

Spiritual Journal

Passage:____**Date:**______

Day 4

Spiritual Journal

Passage:______________________________________**Date:**______

Day 5

Spiritual Journal

Passage:____**Date:**______

Day 6

Spiritual Journal

Passage:____ **Date:**______

Day 7

Notes for Session 6

Session 7

Setting Spiritual Goals

Before You Begin

Share insights from your daily Bible reading.

Someone has said, "If you aim at nothing you'll hit it every time." Unfortunately, many of us have gone for years without targeting clear spiritual goals for our lives. To avoid living this aimless life it is helpful, once or twice a year, to come away from the busyness of life to reassess where you are going spiritually and to set some spiritual goals.

Usually most people do this at either the first of the year, or in the fall as they finish up summer and return to a more active schedule. Many people also reassess their lives and set new goals any time they feel unfocused.

Here are several simple guidelines that many have found helpful:

- Select a quiet place free from distractions, such as a retreat center, an unused classroom at a church, or even your local library.

- Determine the amount of time you want to invest. Usually two to four hours is sufficient. Include within your time one or two refreshment breaks.

▶ Have a plan in mind for how you are going to use the time. Following are some things to consider incorporating into this time of spiritual reflection and assessment:

- Take several minutes to quiet your heart and pray for God's guidance.

- Read and mark a portion of Scripture to focus your mind on the things of Christ. Some have also found it stimulating to read a chapter or two in a spiritual book that focuses on Christian living.

- Have paper and pencil handy to jot down anything the Holy Spirit impresses on your heart while reading, or to jot down to-do items that may come to mind and distract you.

- Review the high points and low points of the last six to twelve months of your life and talk to God about them. This would be a good time for reviewing the previous year's spiritual journal entries to detect any trends in the Holy Spirit's communication to you through the Scriptures. Note any lessons learned, and remember to thank God for his help during those months.

- Ask God to help you establish realistic and concrete goals for your life, your family, your relationships, and your service.

- Close the time praying for the things that God has impressed on your heart and mind during this time and for his help in enabling you to accomplish these goals during the coming months.

▶ Included within these goals should be expectations regarding your commitment to read, meditate, and pray over God's word.

▶ It is always helpful to have a companion with you, for as the Scriptures say, "Two are better than one, because they have a good reward for their toil" (Ecclesiastes 4:9). One of these rewards is mutual accountability that helps you remain faithful to your spiritual resolves. Like New Year's resolutions, if you make them haphazardly and only keep them to yourself, you're more likely to abandon them. However, if you thoughtfully discuss and plan your goals with another who is committed to a similar process and to helping you fulfill them, your chances for success are much greater. Complete the following exercise to get started on bringing focus to your spiritual aim.

WHO: Who can help hold you accountable and share in what you are learning?

____

____

____

____

____

WHAT: What is your plan for utilizing this daily devotional time?

____

____

____

____

____

WHEN: When will you do your daily reading, meditating and praying each day?

WHERE: Where will you read, meditate, and pray?

WHY: Why do you want to develop this discipline and be faithful to this practice?

HOW: How frequently each week will you practice this discipline?

Remember, it is important to be committed to your goals, but you should not be legalistic about them. They are designed to serve you in your objective to become Christlike, not for you to serve them. If you miss a day, or even several days, pick yourself up, dust yourself off, and start again on the journey. You will find over time that you desire to invest more time each day in God's word, that you are becoming more and more consistent, and that God's word is providing essential nourishment for your soul. This will especially be true if you have a companion with whom you can regularly share your journey.

Preparation for Session 8

1. Continue to read and mark your Bible daily, and record your progress on your reading record.

2. After completing your daily Scripture reading each day record at least one reflection in your Spiritual Journal on pages 87-93.

3. Read and mark the information on "Using Devotional Tools" and be prepared to share what you found helpful.

Spiritual Journal

Passage:____ **Date:**______

Day 1

Spiritual Journal

Passage:____ **Date:**______

Day 2

Spiritual Journal

Passage:____ **Date:**______

Day 3

Spiritual Journal

Passage:____**Date:**______

Day 4

Spiritual Journal

Passage:______________________________**Date:**______

Day 5

Spiritual Journal

Passage:____ **Date:**______

Day 6

Spiritual Journal

Passage:____Date:______

Day 7

Notes for Session 7

Notes for Session 7

Session 8

Using Devotional Tools

Before You Begin

Share insights from your daily Bible reading.

Because we are on a spiritual journey of a lifetime, it is important to avoid getting stuck in a rut. We all do, or will, get into a spiritual rut periodically, so it is important to interject some variety into our daily Scripture reading and prayer to get us moving again. In addition to the suggestions we have already given you for ways to enhance your daily Scripture reading and prayer, in this session we would like to introduce several tools which you may find beneficial.

However, a few words of caution should be given before we do. Because these tools have been developed by men and women who have years of spiritual development, they are usually very well done and written in very meaningful ways. Consequently, it is very easy to stop doing any original thinking or praying, and allow other people to do it for us. But tools are not intended to *be* the goal, but the *means* to our goal. The goal that we are concerned about is engaging our hearts and minds in communion with the Lord through the Scriptures and prayer, so that he can communicate with us and transform us into his image. So if you find that these tools are replacing your original thinking, maybe you should set them aside for a later time.

Here are four tools that we recommend:

- **Annual Prayer Journal**—The Spiritual Journal pages that you have been using in this booklet are similar to the pages in the Word Among Us Prayer Journal. The prayer journal provides a half-page entry space every day of the year, plus the Lectionary Scripture reading references, and significant quotes from the Bible or Catholic leaders. Recording your thoughts and/or prayer in one book for each year will make it convenient to review your growth on a regular basis.

- **Devotional Commentaries**—Commentaries are very helpful provided that they stimulate additional prayer and thought about God's word. As we mentioned elsewhere in this study, it is very helpful over time to read an entire book of the Bible during your daily Scripture reading. The continuity of reading chapter by chapter enables you to discover spiritual truths and emphases that you might normally overlook. The Word Among Us has excellent commentaries on each of the Gospels and Acts, and is preparing more commentaries on other New Testament letters. Each is divided into easily digestible portions and recorded in the commentary, followed by succinct and helpful explanations intended to inform and challenge. In light of the above words of caution, we would suggest the following to ensure that you do original thinking:

  - Read and mark the passage as you would in your own Bible.

  - Meditate and pray over the passage as though the commentary was not there.

  - Complete your daily journal entry, either explaining what impressed you or turning your thoughts into a written prayer.

  - After having completed the above, read, mark and think about the commentary.

• Add to your journal entry anything else you feel is significant.

- **Abide in My Word**—If your daily reading revolves around the Lectionary Mass Readings, this tool can be very valuable. *Abide in My Word* is a compilation of the Mass readings tied to each day of the year in an annual paperback volume. Because it is designed for each individual year with all the readings printed out, you can feel free to mark the passages as you read. An added advantage of having the year's readings consecutively marked in one book is that at the end of the year you can peruse what you marked and discover any trends in God's communication with you.

- **A Year of Celebration: Experiencing God through the Feast Days of the Church**—This last tool will enable you to incorporate into your daily Scripture reading some of the celebrations that are uniquely Catholic: the feast days of the Church. This tool identifies the feast days throughout the year and provides the Scriptures that are unique to each feast day. In addition, there is a brief commentary for each day, "Points for Meditation," and a prayer that you can appropriate for yourself. Remember, use this tool with your personal reading, meditation, and prayer. You can also use it at the end of the day to bring your thoughts back to God before you go to sleep.

We hope you will find these and other tools useful as you pursue your lifelong relationship with God. Resolve with Joseph Cardinal Bernardin that "I'm not going to give that time to anybody else. So even though it may not unite me with you as much as it should, nobody else [not even a helpful tool] is going to get that time."

Congratulations!

Completing this study has required dedication and hard work. We are confident that your life in Christ has taken on a new and vibrant dimension, and like a flowering bud, is beginning to open up and blossom into even more beauty and vibrancy. Our prayer for you is that Christ may become the very "apple of your eye."

We would also encourage you to consider continuing on in your spiritual journey by participating in the next small group study, *Embracing the Kingdom.* May God continue to bless you.

Spiritual Journal

Passage:____**Date:**______

Day 1

Spiritual Journal

Passage:____ **Date:**______

Day 2

Spiritual Journal

Passage:____ **Date:**______

Day 3

Spiritual Journal

Passage:____ **Date:**______

Day 4

Spiritual Journal

Passage:____Date:______

Day 5

Spiritual Journal

Passage:____**Date:**______

Day 6

Spiritual Journal

Passage:____ **Date:**______

Day 7

Notes for Session 8

Daily Scripture Reading Record

OLD TESTAMENT

Genesis	1	2	3	4	5	6	7	8	9	10	11	12	13
	14	15	16	17	18	19	20	21	22	23	24	25	26
	27	28	29	30	31	32	33	34	35	36	37	38	39
	40	41	42	43	44	45	46	47	48	49	50		
Exodus	1	2	3	4	5	6	7	8	9	10	11	12	13
	14	15	16	17	18	19	20	21	22	23	24	25	26
	27	28	29	30	31	32	33	34	35	36	37	38	39
	40												
Leviticus	1	2	3	4	5	6	7	8	9	10	11	12	13
	14	15	16	17	18	19	20	21	22	23	24	25	26
	27												
Numbers	1	2	3	4	5	6	7	8	9	10	11	12	13
	14	15	16	17	18	19	20	21	22	23	24	25	26
	27	28	29	30	31	32	33	34	35	36			
Deuteronomy	1	2	3	4	5	6	7	8	9	10	11	12	13
	14	15	16	17	18	19	20	21	22	23	24	25	26
	27	28	29	30	31	32	33	34					
Joshua	1	2	3	4	5	6	7	8	9	10	11	12	13
	14	15	16	17	18	19	20	21	22	23	24		
Judges	1	2	3	4	5	6	7	8	9	10	11	12	13
	14	15	16	17	18	19	20	21					
Ruth	1	2	3	4									
1 Samuel	1	2	3	4	5	6	7	8	9	10	11	12	13
	14	15	16	17	18	19	20	21	22	23	24	25	26
	27	28	29	30	31								
2 Samuel	1	2	3	4	5	6	7	8	9	10	11	12	13
	14	15	16	17	18	19	20	21	22	23	24		
1 Kings	1	2	3	4	5	6	7	8	9	10	11	12	13
	14	15	16	17	18	19	20	21	22				
2 Kings	1	2	3	4	5	6	7	8	9	10	11	12	13
	14	15	16	17	18	19	20	21	22	23	24	25	
1 Chronicles	1	2	3	4	5	6	7	8	9	10	11	12	13
	14	15	16	17	18	19	20	21	22	23	24	25	26
	27	28	29										
2 Chronicles	1	2	3	4	5	6	7	8	9	10	11	12	13
	14	15	16	17	18	19	20	21	22	23	24	25	26
	27	28	29	30	31	32	33	34	35	36			
Ezra	1	2	3	4	5	6	7	8	9	10			
Nehemiah	1	2	3	4	5	6	7	8	9	10	11	12	13

Esther 1	2	3	4	5	6	7	8	9	10	11			
Job	1	2	3	4	5	6	7	8	9	10	11	12	13
	14	15	16	17	18	19	20	21	22	23	24	25	26
	27	28	29	30	31	32	33	34	35	36	37	38	39
	40	41	42										
Psalms	1	2	3	4	5	6	7	8	9	10	11	12	13
	14	15	16	17	18	19	20	21	22	23	24	25	26
	27	28	29	30	31	32	33	34	35	36	37	38	39
	40	41	42	43	44	45	46	47	48	49	50	51	52
	53	54	55	56	57	58	59	60	61	62	63	64	65
	66	67	68	69	70	71	72	73	74	75	76	77	78
	79	80	81	82	83	84	85	86	87	88	89	90	91
	92	93	94	95	96	97	98	99	100	101	102	103	104
	105	106	107	108	109	110	111	112	113	114	115	116	117
	118	119	120	121	122	123	124	125	126	127	128	129	130
	131	132	133	134	135	136	137	138	139	140	141	142	143
	144	145	146	147	148	149	150						
Proverbs	1	2	3	4	5	6	7	8	9	10	11	12	13
	14	15	16	17	18	19	20	21	22	23	24	25	26
	27	28	29	30	31								
Ecclesiastes	1	2	3	4	5	6	7	8	9	10	11	12	
Song of Solomon	1	2	3	4	5	6	7	8					
Isaiah	1	2	3	4	5	6	7	8	9	10	11	12	13
	14	15	16	17	18	19	20	21	22	23	24	25	26
	27	28	29	30	31	32	33	34	35	36	37	38	39
	40	41	42	43	44	45	46	47	48	49	50	51	52
	53	54	55	56	57	58	59	60	61	62	63	64	65
	66												
Jeremiah	1	2	3	4	5	6	7	8	9	10	11	12	13
	14	15	16	17	18	19	20	21	22	23	24	25	26
	27	28	29	30	31	32	33	34	35	36	37	38	39
	40	41	42	43	44	45	46	47	48	49	50	51	52
Lamentations	1	2	3	4	5								
Ezekiel	1	2	3	4	5	6	7	8	9	10	11	12	13
	14	15	16	17	18	19	20	21	22	23	24	25	26
	27	28	29	30	31	32	33	34	35	36	37	38	39
	40	41	42	43	44	45	46	47	48				
Daniel	1	2	[3]	4	5	6	7	8	9	10	11	12	[13]
	[14]												
Hosea	1	2	3	4	5	6	7	8	9	10	11	12	13
	14												
Joel	1	2	3										
Amos	1	2	3	4	5	6	7	8	9				
Obadiah	1												

Jonah	1	2	3	4									
Micah	1	2	3	4	5	6	7						
Nahum	1	2	3										
Habakkuk	1	2	3										
Zephaniah	1	2	3										
Haggai	1	2											
Zechariah	1	2	3	4	5	6	7	8	9	10	11	12	13
	14												
Malachi	1	2	3	4									

DEUTEROCANONICAL BOOKS

Tobit	1	2	3	4	5	6	7	8	9	10	11	12	13
	14												
Judith	1	2	3	4	5	6	7	8	9	10	11	12	13
	14	15	16										
Esther (gr)	1	2	3	4	5	6	7	8	9	10			
1 Maccabees	1	2	3	4	5	6	7	8	9	10	11	12	13
	14	15	16										
2 Macabees	1	2	3	4	5	6	7	8	9	10	11	12	13
	14	15											
Sirach	1	2	3	4	5	6	7	8	9	10	11	12	13
	14	15	16	17	18	19	20	21	22	23	24	25	26
	27	28	29	30	31	32	33	34	35	36	37	38	39
	40	41	42	43	44	45	46	47	48	49	50	51	
Wisdom	1	2	3	4	5	6	7	8	9	10	11	12	13
	14	15	16	17	18	19							
Baruch	1	2	3	4	5	6							
Daniel	3	13	14										

NEW TESTAMENT

Matthew	1	2	3	4	5	6	7	8	9	10	11	12	13
	14	15	16	17	18	19	20	21	22	23	24	25	26
	27	28											
Mark	1	2	3	4	5	6	7	8	9	10	11	12	13
	14	15	16										
Luke	1	2	3	4	5	6	7	8	9	10	11	12	13
	14	15	16	17	18	19	20	21	22	23	24		
John	1	2	3	4	5	6	7	8	9	10	11	12	13
	14	15	16	17	18	19	20	21					

Acts	1	2	3	4	5	6	7	8	9	10	11	12	13
	14	15	16	17	18	19	20	21	22	23	24	25	26
	27	28											
Romans	1	2	3	4	5	6	7	8	9	10	11	12	13
	14	15	16										
1 Corinthians	1	2	3	4	5	6	7	8	9	10	11	12	13
	14	15	16										
2 Corinthians	1	2	3	4	5	6	7	8	9	10	11	12	13
Galatians	1	2	3	4	5	6							
Ephesians	1	2	3	4	5	6							
Philippians	1	2	3	4									
Colossians	1	2	3	4									
1 Thessalonians	1	2	3	4	5								
2 Thessalonians	1	2	3										
1 Timothy	1	2	3	4	5	6							
2 Timothy	1	2	3	4									
Titus	1	2	3										
Philemon	1												
Hebrews	1	2	3	4	5	6	7	8	9	10	11	12	13
James	1	2	3	4	5								
1 Peter	1	2	3	4	5								
2 Peter	1	2	3										
1 John	1	2	3	4	5								
2 John	1												
3 John	1												
Jude	1												
Revelation	1	2	3	4	5	6	7	8	9	10	11	12	13
	14	15	16	17	18	19	20	21	22				

Helping Catholics grow the Church through small groups!

The Emmaus Journey Catholic Small Group Ministry endeavors to stimulate and develop Catholic evangelization by:

- Emphasizing Scripture reading, study, and discussion.
- Ministering within and through Catholic parishes.
- Helping Catholics communicate the essential gospel message.
- Encouraging unity and cooperation in ministry within the body of Christ.

Emmaus Journey

On the Emmaus Journey web page, we offer a *free* downloadable Daily Scripture Reading Record to help you develop consistency in your daily reading of God's word. You will also find additional small group resources and free downloads to assist you in your small group ministry.

In addition, at *The Word Among Us* web page, we offer *free of charge* –

- the Scripture readings used at Mass for each day
- daily meditations and reflections based on the Mass readings
- practical articles on Christian living
- reviews of the newest Emmaus Journey Bible Studies

Please visit our websites today!

Emmaus Journey
www.emmausjourney.org
email: info@emmausjourney.org
phone: 719-599-0448

the WORD among us
www.wordamongus.org
email: theresa@wau.org
phone: 800-775-9673